Star Friends
MYSTIC FOREST

To Eden and Arlo Dawkins – LC
To my brother Richard – KB

LITTLE TIGER
An imprint of Little Tiger Press Limited
1 Coda Studios, 189 Munster Road, London SW6 6AW

Imported into the EEA by Penguin Random House Ireland,
Morrison Chambers, 32 Nassau Street, Dublin D02 YH68

A paperback original
First published in Great Britain in 2023

Text copyright © Linda Chapman, 2023
Illustrations © Kim Barnes, 2023

ISBN: 978-1-78895-625-3

The right of Linda Chapman to be identified as the author and Kim Barnes
as the illustrator of this work respectively has been asserted by them
in accordance with the Copyright, Designs and Patents Act, 1988.

All rights reserved.

This book is sold subject to the condition that it shall not, by
way of trade or otherwise, be lent, resold, hired out, or otherwise
circulated without the publisher's prior consent in any form of
binding or cover other than that in which it is published and
without a similar condition including this condition being
imposed upon the subsequent purchaser.

A CIP catalogue record for this book is available from the British Library.

Printed and bound in the UK.

The Forest Stewardship Council® (FSC®) is a global, not-for-profit organization
dedicated to the promotion of responsible forest management worldwide. FSC
defines standards based on agreed principles for responsible forest stewardship
that are supported by environmental, social, and economic stakeholders.
To learn more, visit www.fsc.org

2 4 6 8 10 9 7 5 3 1

Star Friends
MYSTIC FOREST

Linda Chapman
Illustrated by Kim Barnes

LITTLE TIGER
LONDON

In the Star World

Stardust shimmered and shone on every leaf and every blade of grass and, in a vast forest of tall trees, a wolf, a stag, a badger and a snowy owl gathered round a sparkling pool. In its mirror-like surface, they could see the image of a coastal Devon village with narrow streets and stone cottages.

"Westcombe," murmured the wolf, whose fur was tipped with silver. "It has been a few weeks since we checked on our young friends there."

Hunter the owl swept the tip of one wing over the water. "Reveal the Star Animals and their friends!"

The surface of the pool sparkled even more brightly for a moment and then four different images appeared, each showing a girl and a wild animal with deep indigo eyes.

The stag inclined his majestic antlers towards each pair. "Maia and Bracken," he said, indicating a young fox using his front paws to help an eleven-year-old girl with shoulder-length dark blond hair squash a couple of soft toys and a hoody into an already full rucksack.

"Lottie and Juniper."

He nodded at the red squirrel with bright eyes who was scampering along a curtain rail as a girl with chin-length dark curly hair packed neatly folded T-shirts carefully into a bag.

"Sita and Willow."

A deer with gentle brown eyes was nuzzling a girl with a long, shiny brown plait who was staring from one heap of jumbled-up clothes to another as if she couldn't decide what to take.

"And Ionie and Sorrel."

In the final image, a girl with long strawberry-blond hair tied in a ponytail was pacing anxiously around her bedroom, holding a wildcat with a tabby coat in her arms.

"Our young friends are going on holiday," said the stag. "Maybe they will now have a chance to use the magic current to help people outside their village of Westcombe."

The owl nodded, his eyes wise. "Maia, Lottie, Ionie and Sita have learned a lot since they became Star Friends seven months ago."

Every so often, young Star Animals from the Star World travelled to the human world to try and find a Star Friend – a child who believed in magic. When they found a Star Friend, the Star Animal would show that child how to connect with the magical current that ran between the two worlds. Together, the animal and the child would use that magic to do good deeds and to stop anyone using dark magic.

The owl began to sweep his silvery wing over the water again to clear the pictures.

"Wait, Hunter!" the badger said suddenly. "Is that another person?"

Looking more closely, the animals all saw that the badger was right. In the centre of the pool, a fifth image had formed. The figure was tall and slim, their dark head bent as they kissed the otter snuggled in their arms.

"Well, well, well," said the owl softly. "It appears there is another Star Friend in Westcombe that I do not believe our young friends know yet." He looked round at the other three animals. "Let us watch and see what happens. This could be very interesting indeed."

Chapter One

"All packed!" Maia Greene declared, pulling the drawstring tight on her rucksack.

Bracken, her Star Fox, bounced round her, his eyes bright and his bushy tail with its white tip waving from side to side. "We're going on holiday, Maia!"

"This is going to be the best start to half-term ever," Maia said, happiness bubbling inside her. She had been looking forward to this holiday for ages – three nights staying at a forest camp with her best friends, Ionie, Lottie and Sita.

The holiday information had said that campers would get to do all kinds of forest activities as well as learning outdoor survival skills. When they'd been given a leaflet about the camp at school, Maia, Lottie and Sita had thought it sounded amazing. Ionie had taken a bit more persuading – she'd never been camping before and wasn't sure she liked the sound of the activities – but she also didn't want to miss out on a holiday with her friends so she'd asked if she could go, too. Now the day of their holiday had finally arrived!

Maia's phone buzzed with a text.

We're here! lxx

Maia hurried to the window. Ionie's dad's large seven-seater car was outside the house. Sita, Ionie and Lottie were in the back. Seeing her at the window, they waved wildly.

"It's time for me to go!" Maia said to Bracken.

"See you later," said Bracken, licking her nose as she crouched down to give him a hug. "Make sure you call me as soon as you can!"

"I will!" she promised.

Spinning round, Bracken vanished, leaving just a faint trail of sparkles in the air. Maia smiled. She knew he would come back as soon as she called his name. That was one of the many brilliant things about Star Animals: they had the ability to disappear and reappear whenever they wanted. They tried to avoid being seen by people who weren't Star Friends and so being able to vanish was very useful.

Heaving on her rucksack, Maia wriggled the straps over her shoulders and went downstairs.

Her mum and Ionie's dad were talking by

the front door. Her mum hugged her. "Bye, sweetheart. Have fun."

Maia squeezed her mum tightly then, hearing her friends calling her, she hurried to the car. Ionie's dad followed and put her rucksack in the front with the other bags while she climbed into the back next to Ionie. Lottie and Sita were in the two extra seats in the boot of the car.

"It's holiday time at last!" said Sita excitedly as Ionie's dad started the engine and drove off.

"I hope we get to go climbing," said Lottie.

"And swim in a stream," said Maia.

"And toast marshmallows on a campfire," said Sita.

Maia realized that Ionie was being unusually quiet. "Are you OK, Ionie?" she asked.

Ionie was chewing her lower lip. "I don't know if I want to go after all," she admitted. "What if the food's horrible and there are bugs in our tent?"

"It'll be fine," Lottie told her. "More than fine. It'll be fun!"

"I bet the food will be good," said Maia.

"And we'll get rid of any creepy-crawlies for you," said Sita.

Maia reached out and squeezed Ionie's hand. It was strange seeing her look so worried. In school, Ionie was very confident and in their magic adventures she was usually the first to leap into action. But staying away from home for three nights without parents was quite a big thing and none of them knew exactly what they'd be doing at camp. To Maia, that just made the holiday more exciting, but she knew Ionie liked to know what to expect and she really did hate creepy-crawlies.

"Let's sing something!" Maia suggested to distract her. "How about 'One Hundred Green Bottles'?" She launched enthusiastically into the song.

The countryside sped by. After 'One Hundred Green Bottles', they moved on to songs from when they were little like 'The Wheels on the Bus Go Round and Round', which they kept adding their own verses to.

Maia thought Ionie's dad looked very relieved when they finally arrived at Morkwood Forest.

They drove past a farm with hundreds of chickens pecking around the fields and turned into the forest. They went through the car park for the general public and bumped along a track between fir trees, following the signs until they came to an entrance to a smaller car park with a wooden sign arching over it:

Morkwood Survival Skills Camp

"We're here!" Maia said, excitement whooshing through her as she saw parents and children milling around and talking to people carrying clipboards, who were dressed in green shorts and polo shirts with name badges. "Our holiday's about to begin!"

Chapter Two

Connie Joseph, the camp owner, was standing near the entrance. Her blond hair was in two short plaits and her face was tanned.

"Hi!" she said as Ionie's dad put his window down. "If you could park over by those cones, that would be great, then check in with one of the camp guides."

The guides were dressed in khaki shorts and gilets with lots of pockets. They were ticking names off on their clipboards and helping children carry their luggage over to a circle of logs around a campfire. Beyond the parking area there were a couple of sheds, a huge open-sided yurt with two long tables inside, an outdoor kitchen and a wooden toilet block. Further into the trees, there was an array of tents in a clearing, although they looked very different from the ones Maia had camped in before. Rather than being brightly coloured and made of nylon, they were beige canvas bell tents with sides that could be rolled up.

Ionie's dad began to unload all the bags while the girls scrambled out of the car and breathed in the pine-scented air. The forest looked very exciting, the tall trees clustering together as if they were hiding all kinds of secrets. Maia couldn't wait to call Bracken and see what he thought of it!

"There's Elissa and Harriet," said Sita, pointing to two girls from their school chatting by the campfire.

"And Maddie Taylor," said Ionie, nodding at a tall girl with with long dark brown hair held back by two slides who was sitting on her own. Maddie had joined Maia and Ionie's class six weeks ago.

"There are quite a few people from school here," said Maia, noticing Brad and Tyler from Lottie and Sita's class.

Another car pulled up and three boys from Maia and Ionie's class piled out.

"Hi, you lot!" said Josh, patting his bag and grinning at them. "Hope you're ready to be pranked!"

"If you prank us, we'll get you back!" warned Lottie.

"Come and grab your things, girls," called Ionie's dad.

They were just picking their bags up when an old Land Rover drove in through the gates. A grey-haired woman dressed in wellies and an old green waxed jacket got out and began having a heated conversation with Connie. Connie seemed to be trying to calm her down.

After a few moments, the woman got back into her Land Rover and drove off again, looking cross.

"Everything OK?" asked Ionie's dad curiously as Connie came over.

Connie let out a sigh. "I hope so. That was my neighbour – Mrs Coates. She keeps free-range chickens on the farm that borders the forest. She's not very happy that I've started this camping business here, although I've told her the campers won't disturb her or her chickens. Hopefully, she'll come around soon when she finds we're not going to be a nuisance. This is my first week opening."

After checking in, Maia and the others said goodbye to Ionie's dad and joined the other campers around the fire. Maia was surprised when she saw a familiar adult talking to Maddie – a young woman with braided black hair tied back in a thick ponytail who was wearing the same uniform as the other guides and had a name badge saying: *Ginika Amadi*.

"It's Miss Amadi!" Maia hissed, nudging Ionie.

"What's she doing here?" whispered Ionie.

Miss Amadi was going to be Maia and Ionie's new class teacher when they went back after the half-term break because their usual teacher, Miss Harris, was leaving to have a baby. Miss Amadi had visited the class a few times before school had broken up and Ionie and Maia had decided she seemed nice.

"Hello, girls," Miss Amadi said, looking round and smiling. "Don't look so surprised. I'm still going to be your class teacher! I'm just helping out here this week before I start full-time teaching," she explained. "Connie and I are friends and she asked me if I could provide an extra pair of hands for her first week. I love being outdoors so I jumped at the chance." She patted the log beside her, inviting them to sit down.

"While we're at camp, you can call me Ginni, but when we're back at school you'll have to call me Miss Amadi."

Maia sat down rather shyly next to her. It felt a bit strange having a teacher here and she couldn't imagine calling her Ginni. It just felt wrong!

Connie brought the last of the campers over to the campfire.

Miss Amadi looked at her questioningly. "Did I see Mrs Coates in the car park again?"

Connie nodded. "She's really not happy about us being here."

"I'll take her a peace offering of some chocolate brownies later," said Miss Amadi. "Hopefully she'll calm down soon."

"I really hope so," Connie said. "Anyway time to get started." She banged a small drum and all the campers fell silent. "Welcome to Morkwood, everyone. My name is Connie Joseph and I'm in charge. If you have any worries, do come and see me or go to any of the guides. Their names are Tom, Matt, Emma and Ginni."

As she said their names, each adult stood up and waved.

"Now, time for some camp rules and then we can get on with having fun!"

Connie told them that when she banged the drum it meant they all had to gather round her and she explained where the boundaries of the camp were.

"Definitely no going out of the forest into the fields. The farmer has free-range chickens and doesn't want them disturbed. The other boundaries are marked by red-paint crosses on trees."

She went on to remind them that no mobile phones were allowed and pointed out the tents in the clearing behind the campfire.

"You'll be sleeping in groups of three or four. The five smaller tents in the centre of the camping area are for the camp guides. I really hope you're going to have a wonderful time here, do plenty of fun things and learn lots about the forest. Now, your tents…" Connie checked her clipboard. "Tent One: Jake, Tyler and Brad. Tent Two: Nikhil, Josh and Dan.

Tent Three: Maia, Sita, Lottie and Maddie."

Maia felt as if she'd just had a bucket of ice dumped over her. *Maddie and not Ionie!* She glanced swiftly at her friends and saw they were all looking as shocked as she felt. Ionie's hand had flown to her mouth.

"Tent Four: Ionie, Elissa, Harriet and Anoushka," continued Connie.

Maia hardly listened. Her thoughts were racing. They had to do something! If Ionie wasn't in the same tent as them, they wouldn't be able to have their Star Animals sleeping with them. But it wasn't just that. She also knew how worried Ionie was about camping.

"Take your things to your tents," said Connie when she finished reading out the names. "Then there will be a den-building session and a scavenger hunt before supper."

Ionie looked close to tears. "I don't want to be in a different tent. If I can't be with you, I'm going home!" she said.

"Don't panic. Let's talk to Connie," said Lottie quickly.

But Connie was already deep in discussion with some campers from another school who Maia didn't know. She spotted Miss Amadi heading towards one of the smaller single tents. "Let's ask Miss Amadi instead."

They hurried after the teacher, calling her name.

Miss Amadi stopped by her tent and looked round. "What is it, girls?"

They all tried to explain at once.

Miss Amadi held up her hands. "Whoa! Let me just get my water bottle and then one of you can tell me what's going on."

She ducked into her tent. The entrance flap was rolled up and Maia could see that the tent was very cosy inside. Miss Amadi had an inflatable bed and there was a patterned throw with giraffes laid over her sleeping bag. There was a rag rug on the floor and three wooden crates that were being used as tables with bright scarves draped over them.

"I like your tent," said Sita.

"Thanks." Miss Amadi smiled as she picked up her water bottle from one of the crates. "I've been travelling round the world this year, collecting little souvenirs wherever I go."

She waved at a crate near her bed that had a stand in the shape of a tree with bracelets and necklaces hanging from it, some animal ornaments and a cuddly sloth.

"I always like to make the place I'm staying

in feel like home." She came back out and took a drink of water. "Now, tell me what the problem is."

Maia explained about Ionie not being in the same tent as them.

Miss Amadi looked guilty. "Oh dear, this is my fault. I noticed Maddie sitting on her own and thought she looked lonely so I went to check she was OK. She told me she doesn't really have any friends at school, but she did mention that you'd been friendly, Maia, and that she'd put you down on her application form as someone she'd like to share with. So I asked Connie to swap Maddie and Ionie over. I didn't think you'd mind, Ionie."

"Oh." Maia didn't know quite what to say. She didn't want to upset Maddie but she was really worried Ionie would insist on going home if she couldn't share with them.

"Can they swap?" asked Lottie. "Elissa, Harriet and Anoushka are really nice. I'm sure

Maddie will have fun with them."

"It's not that we don't like Maddie," Maia said quickly. "It's just we really wanted to be together and –" she shot a look at Ionie – "Ionie's a bit nervous about camping."

"If I can't be with the others, I don't want to stay," said Ionie unhappily.

"Oh, Ionie," said Miss Amadi. "If I'd known sharing a tent with Maia, Sita and Lottie was so important to you, I'd never have suggested the swap. Don't worry – I'll sort this out. You and Maddie can change places. But why are you feeling so nervous?"

"I've never been camping before," Ionie admitted. "I'm worried about sleeping in a tent and doing stuff like fishing, and I definitely don't want to have to climb trees. I hate heights."

"If you're really worried about an activity, you won't have to do it," Miss Amadi reassured her. "And we're not just going to do things like climb trees and fish. You'll also learn about the forest, the animals who live here, the tracks they leave, the plants you find. You'll like that, won't you?"

Ionie nodded. She did love learning about things.

"You'll have a wonderful time — I know it. Look."

Miss Amadi glanced round and then went back into the tent and picked up a carved wooden monkey from the crate near her bed. It had a big smile on its friendly face and fluffy ears sticking out of the side of its head.

"My aunt in Nigeria gave this to me when I visited her in the summer. She told me he's very good at looking after people. What do we think, Aaya?" she said, pretending to talk to the monkey. "Will you look after Ionie and help her have a good time while she's here at camp?"

She waggled the monkey from side to side and spoke in a silly voice as if it was answering her. *"Oh yes. Oh yes. I promise I will!"*

Maia exchanged looks with the others. It was really nice of Miss Amadi to try and cheer Ionie up, but they weren't babies!

Miss Amadi bopped Ionie gently on the nose with the monkey and plonked him in her hands. "Here, Ionie, you can keep Aaya while you're at camp and see if he helps."

Ionie managed a faint smile and handed the monkey back. "Thanks, Miss Amadi, but as long as I'm in the same tent as Maia, Lottie and Sita I'll be fine."

"OK, well, let's get that sorted then," said Miss Amadi with a smile. She put the monkey back and led the way over to the girls' tent where

Maddie was just carrying her bag inside.

Maddie looked a little upset when she heard about the swap but Elissa, Harriet and Anoushka came to help her move her things and Maia watched them all walking back across the clearing to Tent Four, chatting and laughing.

"Phew!" she said, letting the flap of their tent close. "Maddie looks happy."

Ionie, Sita and Lottie were laying their sleeping bags out on the thick foam mats that would be their beds for the next three nights. They each had an empty wooden crate with a lid to store their things in and an extra blanket on top. There was a rug on the floor and a groundsheet outside for keeping their muddy boots on.

"And now it's just the four of us like we planned."

Lottie grinned. "Don't you mean the eight of us?" She called Juniper's name.

There was a swirl of starry light and the little

red squirrel appeared. He scampered up the centre pole in the tent. Maia, Ionie and Sita quickly called their animals, too.

Bracken bounced round Maia, while Sorrel wove round Ionie's legs, purring, and Willow cuddled against Sita's side. Bracken jumped into Maia's arms, his soft russet-red fur tickling her chin and his cold black nose pressing against her cheek.

"I like this tent!" said Juniper, taking a flying leap on to Lottie's head and playing with her dark curls. "It's got a climbing pole!"

Sorrel looked round. "Where are the beds?"

"There," said Ionie, pointing to the foam pad where her sleeping bag was.

"You want me to sleep on *that?*" Sorrel said in horror.

"Poor princess pussycat," teased Bracken. "Don't you want to sleep on the ground?"

Sorrel stalked over to the crate beside Ionie's bed. "You can sleep on the ground, Fox, but I –" she jumped up on to the fleecy blanket on top of Ionie's crate – "shall sleep here."

She sat down as if she was on a throne, her nose in the air and her long tail dangling.

Bracken couldn't resist. He darted forward and tweaked the end of her tail with his teeth. Sorrel gave an outraged yowl and leaped up, the fur rising along her back.

"Bracken, don't tease Sorrel!" said Maia,

shaking her head and trying not to smile. Bracken loved to wind Sorrel up.

Ionie soothed the wildcat. "It's OK, Sorrel. Calm down."

Sorrel's coat slowly flattened. Giving a grumpy huff, she curled up like a doughnut on the blanket, glaring at Bracken and wrapping her tail safely round her paws.

They unpacked their things. As Maia took a small round folding mirror out of her rucksack, she paused.

Bracken seemed to read her mind. "Are you thinking of doing some magic, Maia?" he asked eagerly.

Each of the girls could do different things when they connected to the magic current. Lottie could become super agile and sense when the others were in danger. Sita could heal wounds and make people and spirits to do whatever she wanted – although she didn't like that power and only used it at times of real danger. Ionie could shadow-travel and disguise things, including herself, as well as command spirits to return to the realms they had come from. Maia could use shiny surfaces to see things happening elsewhere, get glimpses of the past and the future and create invisible magic shields. Doing magic felt amazing!

"I could have a little look with my seeing magic," Maia said with a grin. "I mean, just to check that there isn't anything magical going on here that we should know about, like someone doing dark magic and summoning Shades."

Shades were evil spirits conjured from the

shadows. They could be trapped in everyday objects and loved to manipulate people and cause trouble and unhappiness. There were all sorts of Shades – Mirror Shades who could make people become jealous; Fear Shades who could terrify people by making them think their deepest fears were coming true; Wish Shades and Heart's Desire Shades who granted wishes but who did it in a way that caused pain and unhappiness to others. There were so many different types and they were all horrible.

Since Maia and the others had become Star Friends, they had sent plenty of Shades back to the shadows as well as stopping people who had been causing trouble, using the magic in plants and crystals.

Maia didn't think for a moment that there would be any bad magic to worry about at camp but she loved doing magic so she sat down on her foam mat with her mirror anyway. With Bracken cuddling up against her, she gazed into the shining surface and silently asked the magic, *Please show me if there is anything magical going on here.*

Her body tingled as the current started to run through her. The trickle of magic became a flood until she felt as if every cell in her body was filled with a wonderful sparkling power. The surface of the mirror began to swirl and images appeared in it! She saw a cute brown otter, the tents in the camp clearing, a woman knocking on a front door in a porch filled with house plants in pots... The images flicked past quickly! An animal with a long tail jumping through the treetops, broken branches and bracken littering a sunny glade of slender firs, a smouldering campfire, two black eyes peering out of lush foliage…

The images faded and Maia lowered the mirror.

"Did you see anything?" asked Bracken eagerly.

"I did," Maia said, unease prickling through her.

The others turned to look at her. "You did?" Ionie said.

Sorrel sat up, suddenly awake. "Well, spit it out, girl. What did you see?"

With the others listening intently, Maia described the images. "I don't know if the things the magic showed me have happened already or might happen in the future."

"Whichever they are, it sounds like there's definitely some magic going on here," Lottie said excitedly.

"The air does smell of it," said Willow, snuffing deeply. She and Sorrel had the ability to smell when Shades were nearby and they were very sensitive to the scent of other magic, too.

"You can smell a Shade?" Sita said in alarm.

Sorrel shook her head. "Not a Shade." She sniffed delicately. "There are a few different kinds of magic, some that seem familiar, but also a magic I do not recognize."

Sita sighed. "Oh, I hope there isn't any bad magic going on here. I just want to have a fun holiday."

"It'll be even more fun if there's magic we have to stop," said Ionie, her green eyes sparkling. "It'll make things much more exciting."

Maia grinned at her. "So you're not still thinking about going home?"

Ionie grinned back. "No way! Not now there's a mystery to solve!"

Chapter Three

A drum banged outside the tent. "That's Connie calling us. We'd better go," Maia said to the animals.

"While you're gone, we'll explore and see if we can find out more about the magic," said Bracken.

"OK, but be careful," said Maia. "Try not to be seen." Although all four animals were the kind of animals that might be found in a forest, Maia was sure the adults would think it strange if they started turning up all the time!

"We will." Bracken put his paws on her knees and licked her nose. "Call us as soon as you can. I'll miss you!"

The girls put on their boots and went to join the rest of the campers.

"It's time for you to learn how to build shelters!" Connie told them. "Emma, Matt and Tom are going to be in charge so make sure you do what they say."

The campers set off with the three guides while Connie stayed in camp to prepare supper and Miss Amadi took some brownies round to the grumpy farmer to try to smooth things over.

Emma, Tom and Matt stopped in a glade surrounded by tall, fir trees at the edge of camp. The sun shone down through the branches, casting tiger stripes of light on the forest floor. Maia frowned. It felt weirdly familiar. She shook her head. It must be her imagination playing tricks on her.

The guides demonstrated how to construct

a frame for a den by tying thick fallen branches together using a variety of knots.

"It's time for you to build your own shelters," said Emma. "You can make a start now and carry on tomorrow. If your shelters are sturdy enough, then anyone who wants to can sleep in their shelter on the final night."

"Do we have to?" said Ionie.

"It'll be fun!" said Emma but Ionie didn't look convinced.

They all set about gathering what they needed. As Maia was pulling a large fir tree branch out of the undergrowth, she caught sight of Bracken's fluffy face peeping mischievously at her from between some brambles. She grinned but waved at him to go away before anyone saw him. Turning, he disappeared into the undergrowth with a flick of his white-tipped bushy tail.

"Emma! I just saw a red squirrel!" exclaimed one of the campers. "It ran up that tree."

"It wouldn't have been a red squirrel, Saffy," said Emma. "They're very rare in Britain and there aren't any in this area."

Saffy looked puzzled. "But it looked really red."

"Grey squirrels often have a chestnut tinge to their coats so that's probably what you saw," said Emma.

"I spotted a little deer," said Elissa. "It was hiding behind those trees."

The girls exchanged alarmed looks. Their animals were really going to have to work harder at not being seen!

"There are all sorts of animals living in this forest," said Tom.

"I just saw a monkey," said Dan.

Tom laughed. "You won't have seen a monkey, Dan. There aren't any wild monkeys in the UK but there are lots of other animals so keep your eyes peeled."

"And look out for their tracks," said Emma. "I found some otter prints by the stream this morning. There's a poster in the yurt with lots of different animal tracks if you want to identify any you find."

Tom clapped his hands. "On with those dens!"

When the structure was finished, the campers started to fill in the sides with leafy branches.

Ionie poked the den she and the others were making. It wobbled alarmingly. "I'm really not sure I want to sleep in that," she said doubtfully. "It looks like it might fall down at any moment."

"You can add some more struts tomorrow and tie everything together more firmly," said Emma, overhearing. "But now it's time for the scavenger hunt!"

She and the other guides handed out a list of things the children had to find, bags to put the items in and walkie-talkies to each team.

"The team who finds the most items is the winner. If more than one team find all the items, it's the first back to camp who wins," Emma said.

"Make sure you stay within the camp boundaries," said Matt. "No going past the red marks on the trees. If you need us, call on the walkie-talkies."

"We'll see you back at the campfire at –" Tom checked his watch – "six o'clock at the latest. Off you go!"

Everyone clustered into their groups.

Maia read out the list. "OK, so we need to find: one grey stone, one white stone, four different leaves, a pine cone, an acorn, a white petal, brown bracken and three different feathers."

"We could call the animals and get them to help," Ionie whispered. "Then we'd be back first and win!"

"Good idea," said Lottie.
"But that would be cheating," protested Sita.

"Sita's right. No magic, OK?" said Maia.

Lottie and Ionie sighed. They were both very competitive.

They set off and spotted the stones they needed in the nearby stream. Then they found three feathers lying on the track. Further down the path there was a clump of old brown bracken.

"How lucky is that?" said Ionie, scooping it up.

"Here. Put everything in the bag, Lottie."

"We still need leaves, a white flower petal, a pine cone and an acorn," Sita said.

There was a rustle in the undergrowth. Maia looked round.

"I bet there are some acorns under the oak trees over there. Come on!" said Lottie. She ran off with Ionie and Sita.

Maia was about to follow when she heard another rustle. Wondering whether it was one of their animals watching them, she went closer and spotted a white flower caught in the brambles. Taking a petal, she paused. It was strange they kept finding everything they needed.

She peered into the bushes.

"Bracken?" she called softly.

"Is that you?" There was a rustle further back in the undergrowth and she saw the branches move.

"Please don't help us. I don't want to win by cheating," she whispered.

There was no more movement or sound. Maia dropped the petal she'd found on the ground. They could find another white flower without Bracken's help.

She caught up with the others and, after a bit of hunting, found the pine cone, acorn and leaves. When they came across a vine with big white flowers they took a single petal and raced back to camp only to find that Dan, Nikhil and Josh had just beaten them to it.

"You're too late!" Josh said triumphantly.

"What took you so long?" teased Nikhil.

Ionie and Lottie looked a bit grumpy.

"How long have you been back?" Maia asked the boys.

"Only about five minutes," admitted Dan. "By the way, you might want to be careful." He glanced at Nikhil and Josh. "When we were going into our tent, we saw a massive beetle crawl into yours."

"A beetle?" echoed Ionie nervously.

"A really big one!" said Nikhil, nodding.

"Yeah, sure," said Maia disbelievingly.

"I don't want to sleep in our tent if there's a beetle in there," Ionie said.

"I bet there isn't really one," said Maia.

"There is and it's huge," said Nikhil.

Ionie squeaked in alarm.

"Well, I'm not scared of beetles," said Lottie.

"Me neither," said Sita. "Let's go and check, Ionie."

They walked over to their tent with the boys following.

"There's absolutely nothing here," said Maia as she, Lottie and Sita raised the foam mattresses and checked under the sleeping bags. "I told you the boys are just…" Lifting her pillow, she caught sight of a huge black beetle as big as her hand. She shrieked and leaped back, hearing an explosion of laughter at the entrance to the tent.

Almost immediately, she realized it was a prank. Her heart slowed down and she grabbed the rubber beetle. "Ha ha! Very funny!" she said, waving it at the boys.

They were clutching their sides. "You're right, it was!" chortled Josh.

"You should have seen your face, Maia!" gasped Nikhil.

Maia saw the funny side and she, Lottie and Sita all joined in with the laughter.

"We'll get you back you know," Maia said, throwing the beetle at Josh's head.

Chuckling, he caught it and the three boys walked off.

"We have really got to prank them back!" Lottie said.

"How?" asked Sita.

"I'm not sure yet but I'll think of something!" Lottie promised.

Chapter Four

At suppertime, everyone sat round the campfire and ate baked potatoes with sausages and baked beans followed by chocolate brownies.

"See, I told you there was no need to worry about the food," Maia said to Ionie as they washed their plates up in a big trough of soapy water and left them on a wooden drying rack. "It's really nice."

"Tonight's was," said Ionie. "But I asked Connie what we're having tomorrow and she said salmon, rice and broccoli. I don't like salmon – or broccoli!"

"Then just eat the rice and pudding," said Maia.

Ionie pulled a face. "She also said we're all going to cook our own supper on the campfire. But what if someone starts messing around near it or stands too close to the flames or the cooking attracts bugs…?"

"Ionie, relax!" said Maia as they went back to the fire. "It'll be fine."

Just then there was the sound of a car pulling into the parking area. The adults looked at each other in surprise.

"I wonder who that is?" Connie said, getting to her feet.

A car door slammed and a woman came stomping towards them. Maia saw that it was the chicken farmer. She had a bulging bag over one shoulder.

"Mrs Coates," said Connie, going to meet her. "Can I help you?"

"You certainly can!" snapped the farmer. "You can help by keeping these children —" she swung her arm round, gesturing at the campers — "away from my chickens!"

"But no one's been near your chickens—" Connie began.

"They most certainly have!" snapped Mrs Coates. "I saw two boys climbing into one of my fields just a few hours ago!"

"Oh my goodness," said Connie in dismay. "I really am very sorry. It must have been during the scavenger hunt." She looked at the campers. "Did someone go out of the forest and into the fields?"

One of the boys Maia didn't know sheepishly put his hand up. "I'm sorry. I think that was me and Anton. We saw a feather in the grass and thought it wouldn't matter if we took it. There weren't any chickens in the field."

"All fields are out of bounds," Connie said. "Do you understand?"

Everyone nodded.

"I'm sorry, it won't happen again," Connie told Mrs Coates.

"It had better not," the farmer said crossly. "And you can take these things back!" She pulled a Tupperware box and a pottery animal out of her bag and pushed them into Connie's hands. "Leaving things by my front door! It's just not on!"

Connie looked confused. "Ginni dropped off the brownies this afternoon. We thought you might like them, but…" She held up the garden ornament – it was a raccoon sitting up on its back legs, holding an acorn made out of a glittering pink crystal. "I've never seen this before in my life."

Mrs Coates snorted and stomped away. Slamming the car door, she drove off.

"Well," Connie said, looking very taken aback, "I have no idea why she thought this had come from us."

She raised the raccoon. It had pricked, pointed, furry ears and shining black eyes that looked beseechingly out from the dark mask-like markings on its face. A long tail curved up behind it and its little human-like hands were holding the pink crystal shaped like an acorn, which had some words engraved on it.

Connie read them out. "*I bring the gift of friendship.*"

Miss Amadi smiled. "Let's not turn that down." She took the raccoon from Connie and placed it on one of the log seats. "If Mrs Coates doesn't want him, he can have a home here."

While the guides handed out sticks, marshmallows, chocolate and crackers so the campers could make s'mores, Maia went over to examine the pottery animal. Earlier on, Willow and Sorrel had said they could smell different kinds of magic, and crystals had magic in them that could be used for good or bad. Could the raccoon's crystal acorn be magical?

Miss Amadi joined her. "He's cute, isn't he?

I wonder how he turned up in Mrs Coates's porch?" She picked up the raccoon. "Well, if the grumpy old lady doesn't want you, I'll keep you!" she said to it. She handed a stick to Maia. "Here you go – it's s'mores time!"

After everyone had made s'mores by squishing toasted marshmallows and chocolate between crackers, Tom and Miss Amadi got their guitars out and everyone sang songs. Even Ionie seemed to enjoy the evening. As the sun set, the solar-powered lanterns in the trees lit up and Connie handed out fleecy blankets to keep them warm.

Despite the chill in the smoky air, Maia felt a glow of happiness as she and the others finally made their way to their tent at bedtime. Each tent also had a lantern outside to light the way.

They sat down on the groundsheet outside and took their walking boots off. Connie had told them to leave them by the entrance flap so that they could find them easily if they wanted to use the toilet in the night. The girls lined their boots up neatly and went inside, turning their torches on so they could see.

"Bed at last!" said Lottie, flopping on to her sleeping bag.

"Let's get into our pyjamas and call the animals," said Sita. "I really want to see Willow."

They got changed and called the animals' names – Bracken, Willow, Juniper and Sorrel – each of them appearing in a shimmer of stars. After enthusiastically greeting the girls, they snuggled down on the beds or, in Sorrel's case, on top of the crate beside Ionie's bed.

"You're really going to have to try harder not to be seen by other people!" said Maia, tickling Bracken's soft, downy tummy as he rolled over on his back on her sleeping bag.

"Yes, Saffy looked very confused when Emma told her there were no red squirrels here!" said Lottie with a grin as Juniper sat on her shoulder, chattering softly.

"And thanks for trying to help with the scavenger hunt today," Maia said to Bracken. "But it's cheating if we use magic in a competition."

Bracken wriggled up, looking surprised. "I didn't help you."

"None of us did," said Willow.

Maia frowned. "So you didn't put the feathers or bracken on the track? Or leave the flower in the brambles for me to find?"

"If you came across things, it certainly wasn't because of us," said Sorrel sharply. "While you were on your hunt, we were busy exploring the camp."

"Did you find anything?" Lottie asked eagerly.

"We did smell magic near the tents," said Willow.

"I think it's stronger now," said Sorrel, sniffing. "Closer."

"Could it be crystal magic you're smelling?" Maia asked, thinking about the raccoon.

"Yes," said Willow thoughtfully. "I did smell crystal magic but also other magic, too. Not Shades though," she said, nuzzling Sita, who looked relieved. "And it might not be bad magic. It could just be someone with crystals or other objects that they don't know are magical."

"Still, someone *could* be planning on doing something bad with magic," said Ionie. "We must keep a lookout."

"Definitely!" said Maia.

"What's happening tomorrow?" Bracken asked. "Can we all go exploring together?"

"I don't think so," Maia said, remembering what Connie had said before they went to bed. "There are lots of activities with the other campers. Tree-climbing and more den-building in the morning, then in the afternoon we're fishing in the stream and learning how to cook on the campfire."

Ionie shuddered. "I don't want to do any of those things. This evening's actually been quite fun, but I'm not looking forward to tomorrow." She looked around. "Or to sleeping in this tent. What if beetles or spiders or mice come in?"

"Don't worry, Ionie," Sorrel reassured her. "If I see a mouse in here, I'll eat it!"

"No!" Maia, Lottie and Sita exclaimed.

"If you see a mouse, you mustn't kill it, Sorrel," said Sita. "Just guide it out of the tent."

Sorrel looked surprised. "But Ionie might like a nice mouse head for breakfast."

"I really wouldn't," said Ionie hastily.

"Ooh," said Lottie suddenly. "Mice! That's just given me an idea for a prank we could play on the boys."

"What kind of prank?" said Maia eagerly.

"I'll tell you tomorrow. I need to see what's in the kitchen first," said Lottie.

Sita yawned. "I'm tired. Let's go to sleep."

"What about our midnight feast?" said Maia.

"Tomorrow," said Ionie, yawning like Sita.

Maia felt a little disappointed but, as she snuggled down further into her warm sleeping bag, she had to admit she was feeling pretty tired, too. "OK, night, everyone," she said as they all turned their torches off.

"Night," the others murmured.

Bracken snuggled into Maia's arms and, burying her face in his soft fur, she fell asleep.

Maia dreamed she was in the forest on her own. Her spine tingled and she swung round, sure something was watching her. She saw a shadow leaping through the tree branches high above. Her heart pounded.

"Juniper?" she called. But the little red squirrel didn't come scampering down the tree.

Maia looked up and saw two small hands holding the branches apart while two black eyes peered at her through the gap in the leaves.

Feeling a wave of alarm, she started to hurry down the forest path. Above her, the creature followed, high up in the trees…

Maia sat up in bed, her heart racing. It was very dark in the tent. She could hear Lottie, Sita and Ionie breathing softly in their sleep. She shook her head to clear the bad dream away, trying to ignore the anxiety that was worming its way up inside her. Her dreams often warned her when there was danger coming.

It might not have been a magical dream, she told herself. *It could have just been a normal one.* She began to snuggle back down in her warm sleeping bag, but stopped when she heard a rustle outside the tent. She froze. It sounded like someone was creeping around out there.

Maia's heart started to race again.

Bracken, who had moved down the bed to sleep by her feet, stirred and sat up. "Is everything all right, Maia?"

"I think there's someone outside the tent," she hissed.

"I'll go and check," said Bracken, vanishing. A minute later, he reappeared. "There's no one there. You must have imagined it."

Maia breathed out in relief. "Phew." She lay down and he cuddled up next to her. She put her arms round him. "I'm so glad you're here with me," she whispered.

Bracken snuggled closer. "I wouldn't want to be anywhere else."

Chapter Five

Maia was woken in the morning by Lottie shaking her shoulder. "Time for breakfast and tree-climbing!"

Maia sat up, rubbing the sleep from her eyes. The sun was coming up, lighting the inside of the tent, and she could feel the fears from the night fading. She pulled on her clothes.

"Where are our boots?" said Sita as they stepped out on to the groundsheet.

They all looked around in surprise. Their boots had gone!

"It's probably the boys playing another prank," said Lottie.

Maia groaned. "I heard a noise outside in the night. Bracken checked but, by the time he got outside, there was no one there."

"What should we do?" said Ionie. "We can't go to breakfast in our slippers." The grass was thick with early-morning dew.

Maia noticed Maddie sitting on the groundsheet of her tent nearby. "Maddie, you haven't seen our boots, have you?" she called.

Maddie shook her head shyly. "Sorry. No."

"It's got to be the boys," said Lottie. "Oi, Dan! Nikhil! Josh!" she shouted at the next-door tent. "Give us our boots back!"

There was a pause and then Dan looked out, his hair mussed up. "What are you lot going on about?"

"Our boots!" said Ionie.

"Can we have them back now, please?" said Sita.

Dan looked confused. "Um…"

"Don't act like you don't know where they are," said Maia, putting her hands on her hips. "We can't get breakfast until we have them."

"But we didn't take them," said Dan. He saw the disbelief on their faces. "Honestly. We didn't."

Maia frowned. He actually looked like he was telling the truth.

"Well, someone did," said Lottie, peering round. "Whoever took our boots, give them back *right now!*" she shouted.

Miss Amadi appeared from the trees behind the tent. "Whatever's going on, girls?" she asked.

They told her about their missing boots. Miss Amadi sighed. "Oh dear, it sounds like a prank."

She went round all the tents. Campers emerged sleepily, in the middle of getting dressed. They all shook their heads when Miss Amadi asked them about the girls' boots.

She came back, looking mystified. "No one has them."

Just then Matt and Tom came through the trees. They were holding four pairs of dripping-wet boots.

"Our boots!" exclaimed Lottie.

"Someone put them in the stream," said Tom.

"We found them when we were fetching water."

"This isn't on," Miss Amadi said, looking round at the campers. "Pranks are all well and good but now Lottie, Maia, Ionie and Sita aren't going to be able to do anything until their boots dry out. Who did this?"

Maia tried to spot someone looking guilty, but no one owned up.

"Pranks like this must stop. Do you understand?" Miss Amadi said.

Everyone nodded.

Miss Amadi turned to Maia and the others. "I'll stuff your boots with newspaper and put them by the embers of the fire to dry them out. If I fetch you some plastic bags, you can put them over your slippers and come to breakfast. I'm afraid you won't be able to join in with the tree-climbing though. You can't do that in your slippers."

Ionie looked very relieved.

Miss Amadi took their boots away and the

girls sat down on the groundsheet.

"What a stupid prank. Now we can't go climbing," said Lottie crossly.

"It would have been fine if whoever did it had just hidden our boots," said Sita. "Why did they have to put them in the stream?"

"Do you think it was the boys?" said Maia.

Lottie shook her head. "They're really annoying at times, but they're not mean."

"What about Maddie?" Ionie said. "She was up before we were. Perhaps she wanted to get back at us because she had to move tents."

"No," Maia said quickly. "I'm sure she wouldn't do something like that. Whenever I've spoken to her, she's seemed nice."

They waited until Miss Amadi came back with carrier bags and tape. She helped them secure the bags over their slippers. As Maia stood up, she noticed a couple of marks on the ground. There was one that looked like a small handprint and a couple that looked like little footprints.

"Are they animal tracks?" she asked Miss Amadi.

Miss Amadi examined them. "Possibly, but I'm not very good at identifying animals from their tracks. They could be from a squirrel or maybe a rat."

"A rat?" Ionie said in alarm.

"It was probably a squirrel," said Maia quickly, not wanting Ionie to be freaked out by the thought of a rat near their tent.

"Oh, *a squirrel*," said Ionie in relief and Maia knew she was thinking about Juniper.

She grinned at her. "Who knows? We may find some fox, deer and cat prints, too!"

They headed over to the yurt for breakfast. Maia had been hoping they'd have sausages again but the fire had been put out overnight for safety reasons and so it was just fruit, muesli and bread.

After breakfast, it was time for tree-climbing near the tents. The guides started off by showing everyone how to climb safely and then the campers had a go. Maia and the others sat with Miss Amadi.

"It's boring just watching," sighed Lottie.

"We don't have to just sit here doing nothing," said Miss Amadi. "I was thinking about Mrs Coates last night and how much better it would be if there could be a friendly relationship between her and Connie. How about we make some toys for her chickens?"

"Toys? For chickens?" Maia echoed.

Miss Amadi nodded enthusiastically. "Chickens love to perch and have things to peck at. We could make chicken gyms from tree branches and fruit-and-vegetable garlands for them to peck at – you can use apples that are bruised, the outer leaves of cabbages and lettuces, things like that. I'm sure we can find that sort of stuff in the store cupboard. What do you think?"

The girls all nodded. It sounded better than just watching the others climb. They found several sturdy branches while Miss Amadi fetched some rope and strong scissors. Then she showed them how to lash the branches together. By break time, they had constructed two jungle gyms and three long fruit-and-vegetable garlands.

"It's a good way to use up fruit and veg that would otherwise be thrown away or composted," said Miss Amadi. "Maybe if Connie and Mrs Coates become friends this could be a regular thing."

After break, they had a lesson on identifying trees and then it was time for more work on their dens. The girls' boots were still damp inside so Connie suggested they put plastic bags over their socks to keep their feet dry inside their boots so they could join in.

With their feet crackling slightly in the plastic bags, they headed to the glade with the other campers. It was a lovely warm day and rays of sunlight were slanting through the tree canopy.

Maia felt very happy. She linked arms with Lottie. "This is great, isn't it?"

Lottie grinned at her. "Yep, I love camping."

"Me too," said Sita. "It's brilliant being outside all the time."

"I've been thinking about the prank to play on the boys," said Lottie. "I saw some wild rice in the store cupboard when we were making the chicken garlands. It's black and looks just like mouse droppings. How about we put some on the boys' beds and pillows?"

Maia grinned. "Oh yes!"

Just then they heard shouting from up ahead. "The dens!"

Maia and the others broke into a run. Reaching the glade, they stopped in shock.

The leafy branches had been pulled from the outside of the shelters, leaving just the structures beneath, the bracken had been hauled out from inside and the glade was now littered with debris.

"Oh no!" cried Sita, running over to where their den had been. Other people's shelters were damaged but theirs was lying in bits on the ground, completely destroyed!

Chapter Six

"Our den's ruined!" said Lottie in dismay, staring at the broken branches.

A memory tweaked at the corner of Maia's mind as she looked round the glade. There was something about the scene that seemed very familiar. What was it?

"Who did this?" Tom demanded. No one put their hand up.

"Maybe it wasn't any of these guys, Tom," said Matt quickly. "They've been with us all morning."

"I was up doing yoga first thing," said Emma. "I didn't see anyone leave their tent before breakfast."

"I guess it could have been people walking through the forest and messing around," said Tom. He sighed. "Looks like everyone needs to start rebuilding."

"I don't think we'll be sleeping in our den tomorrow night," said Lottie as she surveyed the mess of broken branches.

"What a shame," said Ionie, not sounding like she meant it at all.

Sita glanced in Maia's direction. "Are you OK, Maia?"

"Mmm?" Maia said distractedly. She had been looking around, trying to work out why the scene seemed so familiar. Suddenly the penny dropped. "I saw the glade like this when I used the magic current last night!" She pulled the others into a huddle. "This was one of the things it showed me. Do you think that means magic could be to blame?"

"It *is* the sort of horrible thing a Shade would do," Sita said, her brown eyes widening.

"But Willow and Sorrel said they couldn't smell any Shades," Ionie pointed out.

"Maybe one came in the night," said Lottie.

Sita shuddered. "I hope not."

"Come on, guys," said Tom, clapping his hands and coming over to them. "Less chatting, more working!"

Exchanging looks that said *we'll talk about this later*, they carried on with the den.

As Maia sorted the branches into piles of those that could be used again and those that were too broken, she noticed some tracks on a patch of bare ground. They were just like the ones she had seen by their tent that morning – marks that looked like they'd been made by something with little human-like hands and feet.

"Emma!" she called. "What are these?"

Emma examined them. "They're…"

She frowned and
inspected them
from several
different angles.
"You know,
I'm not sure.
Why don't you
have a look at
the poster in the
yurt at lunchtime
and see if you can
find out?"

Maia nodded and, picking up a branch, took another look at the tracks. Was it a coincidence that the same strange tracks had appeared both here and by their tent? Excitement prickled down her spine – or was it a clue?

Maia wanted to talk to the others on their own but, when they got back to camp, they were ushered straight into the yurt for a lunch of crisps, sandwiches and fruit. Spotting the poster that had pictures of different animal tracks, Maia went over to examine it.

There were no tracks that matched the ones she'd seen. The handprints were a little like the tracks rats and squirrels made with their front paws, but the footprints were different. In the tracks Maia had seen, the foot had a big toe that looked almost like a thumb. She frowned. What could have made them?

Miss Amadi came over, pulling her out of her thoughts. "I took the chicken toys and garlands to Mrs Coates before lunch."

"Did she like them?" Maia asked.

Miss Amadi pulled a face. "Hard to tell. I think she was surprised. She said a quick thank you and then shut the door, but maybe the friendly gesture will help." She sighed. "I really hope it does."

Maia was eager to talk to the others about the tracks and about having seen the glade with the dens destroyed in her dream but, as soon as lunch was finished, Miss Amadi organized a game of rounders. Then they all had to go to the stream with Emma, Matt and Tom to learn how to fish.

I'll talk to them before supper, Maia thought.

To their relief, the only fish they caught were little sticklebacks that they were told to immediately release again. At five o'clock, everyone headed back to the camp to cook salmon, bought in the supermarket, over the fire.

"Connie should have the fire going by now – it needs to be good and hot to cook on," Emma said as they walked through the trees.

"Is that smoke?" Matt said, pointing in the direction of the camp. Looking up, they saw a big cloud billowing above the tree canopy. The guides exchanged alarmed looks.

"I'll stay here with the campers. You go ahead and see what's going on," Emma said to Matt and Tom. They nodded and sprinted off.

"OK, keep calm, everyone!" Emma called. "I'm sure everything's fine, but we'll just wait here for now."

"What if it's a fire?" Ionie said in alarm.

"Then we'll follow the fire procedure, evacuate from camp and call the fire brigade," Emma said. "Don't worry."

A few minutes later, they heard Matt shouting to them. "It's OK! You can all come back — it's safe!"

They hurried through the trees and saw that the campfire was now a smoking heap of damp logs. Maia stopped in her tracks. She'd seen the smouldering campfire with her magic just like she'd seen the destroyed dens!

Two large barrels were lying on their sides next to the fire. Connie and Miss Amadi were standing with Tom and Matt. They were all shaking their heads and looked shocked.

"What happened?" Emma exclaimed.

"The water barrels that collect rainwater

tipped on to the fire, putting it out," said Matt.

"I was in the kitchen area when I heard a huge bang," said Connie. "I came out and saw this!" She waved at the fire.

Miss Amadi frowned. "But how can the barrels have just fallen over?"

"They can't have done," said Tom grimly. "Someone must have pushed them. Maybe the same person who wrecked the dens."

Connie rubbed her forehead, looking very upset. "Why would anyone do such horrible things?"

Miss Amadi hugged her. "I've no idea."

"It's almost like someone is trying to sabotage the camp," said Matt.

The adults exchanged worried looks.

"What should we do?" said Connie.

"I suppose all we can do is get the fire started again and keep a lookout for anything else happening," said Miss Amadi.

Emma nodded and turned to the campers. "OK, everyone, we need to collect lots of wood to get the fire going."

"It won't be hot enough to cook on tonight," said Connie, "so it'll be takeaway pizza for supper."

There was a chorus of delighted cheers. It seemed that Ionie wasn't the only one who hadn't been looking forward to salmon for supper!

As everyone began collecting sticks, Maia pulled at the others' arms. She couldn't wait to talk to them any longer. "We need to speak!" she hissed. "Right now!"

Chapter Seven

Maia was almost bursting with the news by the time they got back to their tent. They called the animals and the words tumbled out of her. "I saw the glade with the wrecked dens and the smouldering campfire yesterday with my magic! I think the adults are right and someone's trying to cause trouble here at camp, and I think they're doing it by using dark magic."

Sorrel hissed, Willow pawed the ground and Juniper chattered uneasily.

"What kind of dark magic?" Sita said.

Bracken put his paws on Maia's knees. "Maia, you could use your magic to look back into the past at the dens being destroyed and the campfire being put out and see what happened."

"OK."

Maia got out her mirror. Cupping it in her hands, she tried to clear her mind so that she could connect with the magic current, but her thoughts were churning – the fire, the dens, the boots. She frowned as the surface of the mirror stayed stubbornly mirror-like.

Bracken leaned against her. "Relax. Remember you can't connect to the current if your mind's too busy. Stroke me."

Maia smoothed his soft fur and breathed deeply. Her thoughts began to clear and this time the current tingled and sparked through her and the mirror swirled.

She saw a small, shadowy figure darting between the dens. Maia frowned. It seemed to be moving on four legs and was that a furry long tail? Branches whizzed across the glade until the movement suddenly stopped and all that was left were the damaged and destroyed dens. The image changed to the campfire. She saw the barrels being  tipped over one after the other and then, just for the briefest of moments, she glimpsed a small face with dark eyes and fluffy ears. A memory stirred in her mind, but then it was gone.

Maia lowered the mirror and told the others what she had seen.

"It sounds like a Shade," said Bracken. "They move really fast."

"But we couldn't smell any Shades yesterday when we looked around," said Willow.

"Maybe that's because it wasn't here yesterday," suggested Ionie.

Sorrel nodded.

Maia picked up her mirror again. She'd had an idea. *Show me if a Shade is doing all these things here at camp*, she thought.

The mirror swirled but no picture appeared.

"What can you see?" Bracken asked.

"Nothing. But there could be some kind of blocking spell."

People using dark magic could perform such spells so that they couldn't be spied on.

Maia frowned. "Though usually…" She shook her head and broke off. Usually she saw a dark cloud, not just nothing like this, but maybe that wasn't important. She decided not to mention it. "No, it doesn't matter. It must be a blocking spell."

"If there is a Shade, who conjured it?" Lottie said.

"And why? Who'd want to cause trouble

here in camp?" said Sita.

"I know!" Ionie exclaimed. "Mrs Coates!"

Maia caught her breath. Of course! The bad-tempered farmer wanted the camp to fail. She had a reason for ruining things. Maia grabbed her mirror. "Show me Mrs Coates with anything magical!"

A picture immediately appeared of Mrs Coates in the porch of her house with a bag over one shoulder. There were house plants on shelves and wellies by the door. Maia saw her march out of the porch and get into her Land Rover.

"It *is* Mrs Coates!" Maia exclaimed.

"Did you see what object the Shade is trapped in?" Bracken asked eagerly.

"No. But it could have been in the bag she was carrying," said Maia.

Sorrel paced round the tent. "We need to find out what that object is – and where it is."

Juniper leaped on to Lottie's head. "But how?"

They heard the drum banging. "It's suppertime," said Sita.

"Let's think up a plan at bedtime," said Maia.

They all nodded.

Maia jumped to her feet, feeling a rush of determination. Wherever the Shade was, whatever it was hidden in, they would find it and stop it before it did anything else!

As they made their way to the campfire, Lottie whispered to the others, "Are we still going to prank the boys into thinking mice have been in their tent?"

"We might as well," said Maia.

Lottie grinned. "Cool! I'll get some rice from the store."

The pizza was delicious. While everyone was clearing away, Lottie pulled the others to one side. She had slipped into the store and her pockets were now bulging with rice.

"Sita, can you and Ionie make sure the boys don't come back to their tent?" she whispered. "Maia and I will set the prank up."

Lottie and Maia ran to the boys' tent and scattered the wild black rice across their sleeping bags and up on to the crate where they were keeping their midnight feast. It looked just like mouse droppings!

"Final touches," said Lottie, picking up a chocolate bar and nibbling at the wrapper with her teeth.

Maia giggled. It looked like an army of mice had been having a party in the tent!

Lottie placed a few grains of rice near a cuddly animal on one of the beds. "All done."

"Wait!"

Maia's attention was caught by the toy. It was a fluffy raccoon. Another raccoon popped into her head – a pottery raccoon with a long tail, large eyes in a mask-like face and little front paws – paws that would make prints that looked almost like tiny human hands…

She gasped. "Lottie! I think I know what Mrs Coates has trapped the Shade in!"

Chapter Eight

Maia and Lottie raced out of the tent. They charged over to the others who were hovering near the edges of the campfire. Everyone else was starting to sit down and get ready to toast marshmallows. Maia beckoned Ionie and Sita over and pulled them into a huddle, then she told them what she'd just worked out.

"The pottery raccoon?" Ionie whispered, her eyes wide. "You think Mrs Coates trapped the Shade in that?"

Maia nodded. "It fits! I had a dream where

I saw an animal with little hands and big round eyes following me through the forest. And I saw some strange tracks near our tent and by the dens. I think they could have been made by the raccoon."

"So the Shade stole our boots?" said Sita. "As well as destroying the dens and putting out the fire?"

Maia nodded.

Lottie frowned. "But why? How would stealing our boots wreck the camp?"

"I don't know," Maia said impatiently. "Maybe it was going to steal everyone's boots, but it got disturbed. It's the raccoon. I'm sure it is! Mrs Coates is the only person who wants the camp to fail and the bad things all started happening *after* she left the raccoon here."

"Hang on," said Ionie suddenly. "Mrs Coates told us she'd found the raccoon in her porch. She said it wasn't hers."

"She must have been lying," Maia said.

"Pretending so she had an excuse to leave the raccoon here."

They all nodded.

"We need to find that raccoon," said Ionie.

"Miss Amadi said she was going to keep it," said Maia. "It's probably in her tent."

"Then let's get it while she's at the campfire with the others!" said Ionie.

"Wait! We'll get into loads of trouble if someone sees us going into Miss Amadi's tent," said Sita.

Ionie grinned. "Then let's not be seen. We can shadow-travel in!"

When Ionie connected to the magic current, she could move from place to place by moving through shadows and she could take the others with her if she was holding their hands.

"Maia, why don't you come with me? Lottie, Sita, you keep guard. If Miss Amadi gets up from the campfire and looks like she's heading for her tent, then distract her."

"OK!" Lottie and Sita agreed.

Ionie turned to Maia, her eyes shining. "Are you ready for some fun!"

"Definitely!" Maia replied.

They ran into the nearby trees where the shadows were dark. Ionie took Maia's hand. "Here we go!"

She shut her eyes and suddenly Maia felt as if the world was falling away. She had the sensation of spinning round very quickly in space and then her feet bumped into the ground.

Her eyes blinked open. They were in Miss Amadi's tent and it was very dark. She could just make out the glow of the solar-powered lanterns on the ground outside.

"Torches!" Ionie hissed.

They pulled them out of their pockets and switched them on. The teacher's tent looked just as it had before, the throw pulled over the bed, ornaments and trinkets neatly arranged on top of the upside-down crates. Maia flashed her torch over them, her gaze darting across the ornaments — a brass elephant, a bowl of crystals, the carved monkey Miss Amadi had been silly with, a silver otter, lots of necklaces and rings and the stuffed toy sloth. However, there was no sign of the pottery raccoon with the pink crystal in its hands.

Ionie searched behind the crates and Maia looked under the throw on the bed and flashed her torch round the edges of the tent.

"It's not here," Ionie whispered.

Suddenly they was a loud yell outside the tent.

"Ow! Ouch! Ow!" they heard Lottie shouting dramatically. "My ankle!"

"Oh my goodness, Lottie, are you OK?" came Miss Amadi's voice.

"Miss Amadi!" Maia hissed. "We've got to get out of here!"

Ionie grabbed her hand and Maia felt the magic carrying them away. They stepped out of the shadows in the trees just in time to see the other campers heading off to their tents for the night. Lottie and Sita were with Miss Amadi. Sita spotted Ionie and Maia and nudged Lottie. Immediately Lottie's hobbling grew less.

"Oh, it's getting better," she said to Miss Amadi.

"Are you sure you don't need me to strap it up?" Miss Amadi said in concern.

"No thanks – I'll be alright," said Lottie. "I must have just twisted it."

Maia and Ionie hurried over. "Are you OK, Lottie?" Ionie asked innocently.

"Yes, I'm fine," said Lottie, hiding her grin.

Just then there was a yell from Dan, Nikhil and Josh's tent and the three boys came scrambling out. "Miss! We've got mice in our tent!" exclaimed Dan, seeing Miss Amadi.

"They've pooed on all our things!" said Nikhil.

Miss Amadi sighed. "Let me have a look." She shone her torch in through the flap. "Oh dear." She ducked inside and then they heard her start to chuckle. "Boys, I don't think you've got mice," she said as she came out, smiling.

"What?" Dan said. "But there's mouse poo everywhere!"

"Ha! Pranked you!" said Maia, high-fiving Lottie.

"It's not poo – it's just rice!" said Lottie, giggling.

"What?" exclaimed Josh.

"Got you!" said Lottie.

The boys ran back into the tent. "It *is* rice!" they heard Nikhil say.

The boys came out, laughing. Miss Amadi joined in.

"Good trick, girls. OK, everyone, time for bed now."

Grinning at each other, the girls went into their tent.

Once camp was quiet, Sorrel and Willow went to see if they could sniff out the Shade. Meanwhile Maia tried her magic again. She knew it wouldn't show her the Shade, but she'd thought of something else she could try. Holding the mirror, she whispered, "Please show me where the raccoon ornament is."

The mirror swirled and she saw two dark eyes peeping out from behind wide, glossy leaves and narrow green leaves with a pale stripe.

"I can see plants," Maia said. "It must be hiding in the forest." She frowned as she studied the picture. What kind of forest tree had leaves like that?

Sorrel and Willow came back into the tent. Maia lowered the mirror.

"Did you find the Shade?" Ionie asked.

"No," said Sorrel. "We couldn't smell it at all."

"The magic's just showed me that it's in the

forest," said Maia. "It might be too far away for you to smell."

"Or it might not be a Shade," Willow said.

"It's got to be," said Maia. "I saw it moving really fast like Shades do and it's making horrible things happen."

"Causing chaos and trouble," said Juniper, nodding. "Just like a Shade."

Sorrel flexed her claws. "I think we animals should watch over the campsite tonight. If it tries anything, we'll wake you."

"And then we'll catch it!" Ionie exclaimed.

Maia nodded determinedly. "And save the camp!"

Chapter Nine

That night, Maia dreamed she was in the forest. She was being followed by something. The leaves were rustling and she could see a shadowy shape jumping from branch to branch in the trees. Her heart sped up. What did it want? Why was it following her? She started to run but tripped on a tree root. As she lay sprawled on the ground, she looked up and saw a little face with dark markings around its eyes and round fluffy ears peering at her through the thick green leaves…

Maia woke up. She could hear birds outside and could tell from the light that the sun was rising. She sat up in bed and saw Bracken lying by the tent entrance, his head poking out under the flap.

"Bracken!" she whispered.

He pulled his head back in and took a running leap on to the bed. She cuddled him.

"Is everything OK?"

"Yes," he said. "The campsite's been quiet all night. Juniper went out earlier and checked the dens and they haven't been touched."

Maia felt a rush of relief. "Phew!"

"What activities have you got today?" Bracken asked.

"A treasure hunt this morning," said Maia, remembering what Connie had told them the night before. "Then this evening we're having a quiz competition. Oh, and this afternoon we're going to a river outside the camp to swim and climb the rocks."

"I really don't want to do that!" said Ionie, waking up and overhearing. "What if the Shade decides to try and hurt someone while they're climbing?"

The thought had crossed Maia's mind, too. It would be the perfect opportunity for the Shade. "We'll stay alert," she said.

They got dressed, said goodbye to their animals and went to have breakfast. Maia pushed the muesli round in her bowl. She didn't feel hungry even though they hadn't eaten their midnight feast the night before. None of them had felt like it – they'd been too worried about the Shade.

After breakfast, each team was given a map and a list of clues, which – if solved – would lead them to their own box of treasure.

Maia and her friends set off into the trees. The chatter of the other groups faded until they were just left with the sound of birds singing and the crunch of their feet on pine needles. A butterfly fluttered past Maia's nose. If she hadn't been feeling so on edge, she would have really been enjoying going on a treasure hunt in the forest but, as they went deeper into the trees, her feeling of foreboding grew.

Ionie and Lottie led the way, reading out the clues. Maia didn't really pay attention – she was too busy scanning the treetops. Maybe it was because of her dream the night before but she had the distinct feeling they were being spied on. Overhead, a tree branch shook. She glanced up and gasped as she caught a glimpse of something jumping through the air.

"What's up?" said Ionie, looking round.

"There's something in the trees," Maia said. "I think it's following us."

"I'll go and check," said Lottie.

She took a deep breath, connecting with the current, and then began to climb a nearby tree. Using the magic, she was as agile as a squirrel. They watched as she got higher and higher before coming to rest on a branch and looking all around. She shook her head at them, then swiftly climbed down.

"I couldn't see anything."

Maia bit her lip. "I'm sure the raccoon is up there somewhere. I think we should call the animals. They can vanish if anyone comes. Bracken!"

The others joined in. "Juniper!"

"Sorrel!"

"Willow!"

The animals were there in a second.

"Has something happened?" Sorrel asked Ionie.

"Not yet but Maia thinks we're being followed," she replied.

"I went into the trees but I couldn't see anything," said Lottie.

"Let's keep going," said Maia. "But be careful!"

They set off again with the animals at their sides. Every rustle made them jump and look round. Maia was very glad she had Bracken there. She had just paused to stroke him when an acorn fell from above, almost hitting her. Glancing up, she saw two eyes peering at her from between some leaves.

"There!" she cried, pointing.

The face vanished. Maia saw the leaves rustling ahead of them and knew the raccoon must be leaping from branch to branch. She set off deeper into the trees after it.

"It's going that way! Come on!" she shouted.

They all charged after her, jumping over roots and rabbit holes. As they ran, Maia felt something niggling at the back of her mind. The creature's face hadn't looked quite right, but she couldn't work out why.

"We've gone past the boundary of the camp!" Sita exclaimed.

"Who cares?" panted Ionie. "We have to catch it!"

"I'm faster than any of you if I use magic," said Lottie. "I'll get it!"

"No! Wait!" said Sita. "I know what to do!"

She stopped and shouted up into the trees. "Spirit, I command you to come down!"

"Brilliant idea, Sita," breathed Maia as the trees stopped rustling.

"Get ready to grab it and send it back to the shadows," said Sorrel.

They waited with bated breath as a small creature with a long tail emerged from the tree canopy and began to climb down the tree trunk.

Something wasn't right. Maia realized it instantly. The animal had a plain tail, not a stripey one like a raccoon, and its body was a different shape. It stopped at the base of the trunk and turned round to look at them. As Maia saw its face, she felt a lurch of shock. It was the monkey from Miss Amadi's tent!

"That's not the raccoon!" said Ionie in astonishment.

"It might not be but the Shade's inside it!" Maia cried, leaping towards the monkey. The others followed her. "Come here, you ... argh!" Maia shrieked as the ground suddenly gave way beneath her feet. The branches they had just run over had been disguising a deep pit!

They tumbled into it, their arms flailing, before they landed on a pile of leaves and heather.

"Maia, are you OK?" asked Bracken, jumping up and licking her face.

"Yes, I'm fine," she said, sitting up and feeling

relieved when she saw the others sitting up, too. Lottie was rubbing her head as if she'd banged it, but everyone else looked uninjured.

The monkey peered over the edge of the pit and smiled broadly. "Good!" it said, sounding very pleased with itself. "My plan worked. Now you won't have to go rock climbing."

Maia felt a rush of confusion. *Rock climbing?*

"What are you talking about, you silly creature?" hissed Sorrel. "And why have you put us in this … this dirty hole!" Her whiskers quivered with outrage.

"Temper, temper! I'm just doing what I was told and making sure that *she* –" the monkey pointed at Ionie – "has a good time at camp."

"What do you mean?" Maia demanded.

"That was the instruction I was given when the Star Magic woke me up and I've been carrying it out ever since," the monkey said. "And doing very well, if I say so myself. I've been popping out of Ginni's tent whenever

I've been needed. I helped Ionie find the things she wanted on the scavenger hunt, I got rid of her boots so she wouldn't have to climb trees, I destroyed the den so she wouldn't have to sleep in it and I put out the fire so she wouldn't have to cook on it." It turned a somersault. "I've been a very helpful monkey!"

Maia stared at it. "You mean, everything that's happened was because of Ionie?"

"And it wasn't Mrs Coates trying to sabotage the camp?" Lottie burst out.

"Mrs Coates?" said the monkey, looking puzzled. "Who's she?"

Maia could hardly believe it. They'd got it so wrong!

"Hang on," Ionie said suddenly. "What do you mean Star Magic woke you up?"

The monkey looked surprised. "You should know – you were there. When I felt the touch of Star Magic, I woke up and heard the instruction to make sure you had a good time. That's what I've been doing ever since."

"I don't understand this. Are you some kind of Wish Shade?" asked Sita.

The monkey slapped its legs and chuckled. "Me? A Wish Shade? Oh no!"

Ionie stared the little animal straight in the eyes. "Well, whatever kind of Shade you are, I am a Spirit Speaker with the power to command spirits to return to their own worlds. I command you to return to the shadows where you belong!"

They waited for the Shade to shriek in annoyance and spiral out of the monkey, but nothing happened.

"Why is it not going back to the shadows?" Ionie asked Sorrel.

"Because it's not a Shade," said Sorrel, her indigo gaze fixed on the monkey who was chuckling to itself. "It is a different kind of spirit altogether."

"The Star Cat is correct. I am a Jeniyan Spirit from the Realm of Light," said the monkey, waggling its ears. "A good spirit who helps people." It gave them a cheeky grin.

"Oh no," groaned Bracken, covering his muzzle with his front paws. "I've heard of good spirits like this. They can cause just as much trouble as Shades. They might not mean to, but they do."

"I don't cause trouble," the monkey said indignantly. "I help people!"

"Do you think you could help us out of this pit?" said Ionie hopefully.

The monkey shook its head and backed away. "Oh no, no, no. If I did that, you would have to go rock climbing and you might also eat the poisoned sweets."

"The *what*?" Maia said, feeling her stomach drop.

"Poisoned sweets?" echoed Sita.

"Yes, I'm off to poison the sweets in those treasure boxes!" said the monkey cheerily.

"But why?" gasped Maia.

"So that everyone who eats them will get sick, then they won't be able to take part in the quiz competition and Ionie will win. I know she likes to win things." The monkey beamed.

They all spoke at once.

"No! You mustn't!"

"You can't poison people!"

"I don't want to win that much!" Ionie cried.

"Don't worry!" The monkey turned another somersault. "The plant poison I'm using won't kill the other campers. It'll just make them very sick for a night. The adults will be fine as long as they don't eat the sweets, which means they'll still be able to run the quiz so you can win. I'll be back once I've got round all the treasure boxes!" It waved its tail at them. "*Byeeee!*"

"Wait! I command you to stop!" cried Sita.

The monkey had its fingers in its ears and was singing loudly. "*La-la-la-la-la!* Can't hear you, Commanding One!"

"We've got to do something!" Maia cried. "Lottie, can you get out of this pit?"

"I'm feeling a bit dizzy," admitted Lottie. "I bumped my head when we fell in here." She looked up to where a tree root was sticking out of the pit wall. "But if Sita could heal me, and someone could give me a leg-up, then I could try and reach that root and then…"

"It's escaping! There isn't time!" said Ionie as the monkey jumped away from the edge of the pit. "Quick! Maia, hold this for me!" She grabbed a large fir branch off the floor of the pit and held it up like an umbrella.

"What? Why?" said Maia, taking it.

"We have to stop that monkey right now!" said Ionie. And, jumping into the small patch of shadow under the fir branch, she vanished!

Chapter Ten

There was a moment's stunned silence in the pit and then Sorrel vanished, too, and they heard Ionie shouting. "You stop right there, monkey! You're not going to ruin camp for everyone! You are not to put poisoned sweets in the treasure boxes!"

Maia pulled the mirror out of her pocket. "Show me what Ionie's doing!"

A picture appeared and Maia watched intently.

"The monkey's scrambling a tree," she told

the others. "Oh my goodness, Ionie's going after it!"

"But she's scared of heights!" Lottie burst out.

"I guess she knows she won't be able to command it to return to its own world unless she's looking into its eyes," Maia said. "Sorrel's with her. They're both climbing the tree."

"Sita, can you use your magic to stop me feeling dizzy?' said Lottie.

Sita nodded. She put her hand gently on Lottie's head and connected with the current as Maia continued to describe what she could see as she watched Sorrel overtake Ionie and claw her way up the oak tree, determination on her tabby face. The monkey started to talk and Maia lifted the mirror closer to her so she could hear what it was saying.

"I thought you didn't like climbing trees, Ionie, but it's fun, isn't it?" she heard the monkey say gleefully as Ionie edged up the tree.

Maia saw Sorrel veering off along a branch underneath the monkey. The cat crawled across it and then her muscles tensed and she leaped through the air, landing on the next tree along, her sharp claws digging into the trunk to stop herself from falling.

The monkey was too busy watching Ionie to notice her. "You're almost up as high as me now,

Ionie!" it said encouragingly. "I'm glad you've finally realized how much fun climbing is!"

"I am not climbing for fun! I'm going to get you and I'm going to stop you!" Ionie panted as she hauled herself on to a thick branch that was level with it.

"Ow!" she winced as an overhanging branch scratched her cheek. Ignoring the scratch, she struggled further along the branch until she was sitting astride it, her back to the trunk, her legs wrapped round the branch.

"Shall we play tag now you're up here!"

cried the monkey. It turned to swing away and then shrieked in shock as it came face to face with a very angry Sorrel who had snuck up behind it. She swiped at it with her paw and it leaped backwards, falling straight into Ionie's arms.

"Got you!" Ionie cried, wobbling precariously as she held it by the scruff of its neck. The monkey struggled but she hung on grimly and looked it straight in the eyes. "Jeniyan Spirit, I command you to return to the Realm of Light!"

For a moment, the monkey's eyes sparkled incredibly brightly and then they dulled as the spirit returned to its own realm and it became just a plain wooden ornament again.

Maia saw the relief cross Ionie's face. She sagged back against the trunk but then glanced down and seemed to realize how high up she was. The relief on her face turned to fear and she clung to the tree trunk. She looked too scared to move and the scratch on her face was bleeding.

"Ionie's sent the spirit back to its own world," Maia said in alarm. "But now she's stuck in the tree! She looks terrified."

Juniper leaped around anxiously. "We need to help her get down, Lottie. Are you feeling better now?"

"I'm completely back to normal," said Lottie, throwing a smile at Sita. "Thanks, Sita!"

"No problem," said Sita. "Do you think you can help Ionie?"

Lottie jumped to her feet. "I'm sure I can. Maia, can you give me a boost up?"

"Sure." Maia cupped her hands together.

Lottie took a deep breath, connecting to the current, and then she stepped on to Maia's hands and sprang upwards, her hands grabbing for the tree root that was sticking out of the pit wall above their heads. She swung from it for a moment building up momentum and then somersaulted effortlessly out of the pit. Juniper vanished and reappeared beside her at the top.

"Good luck!" called Maia.

"Get Ionie down safely!" begged Sita.

Maia used the mirror to watch as Lottie started to climb the tree Ionie was in. Sorrel had edged along the branch until she was beside her Star Friend.

"It will be all right," she was saying. "Lottie and Juniper are coming." Her usually sharp voice was soothing. Ionie let go of the branch with one trembling hand and stroked her.

"I'm glad you're here with me, Sorrel," she said shakily.

"You are incredible," Sorrel told her. "So brave. You stopped the monkey from poisoning everyone, now you just need to stay brave so you can get down the tree. Lottie and Juniper are coming to help. No, don't look at the ground," she said firmly. "Just keep looking at me."

Ionie nodded and continued to stroke her, her eyes fixed on Sorrel's dark blue ones.

Maia saw Lottie and Juniper reach them. "OK, I'm going to guide your feet down,"

Lottie said. "Put your weight where I say."

"I'll guide your hands," said Juniper.

"And I'm here right beside you," said Sorrel. She rubbed her head against Ionie's cheek. "You can do this, Ionie."

Ionie took a deep breath and nodded.

Little by little, Lottie, Juniper and Sorrel helped her down the tree until her feet were finally back on solid ground.

Maia hugged Sita. "She's safe!" she exclaimed as Ionie sagged against the trunk. She turned back to the mirror.

"That was really scary!" Ionie said.

"But you did it," said Lottie, hugging her. "You were so brave going up there after the monkey, particularly when you're scared of heights."

Sorrel rubbed her head against Ionie's arm, purring proudly.

"There was no way I was going to let it poison people," said Ionie. She put a hand to her bleeding cheek. "Ow."

"We need to get Maia and Sita out from the pit," said Lottie.

"Please do!" Maia shouted up to them.

"Do you think we can make a rope from creepers?" Lottie asked Ionie.

"No need." Ionie straightened up. The next moment, Maia and Sita saw her look over the edge of the pit. "Get that fir branch ready to make some shadows, Maia," she grinned, looking much more like her normal self. "I'm coming in!"

In next to no time, Ionie had shadow-travelled into the pit and shadow-travelled them back out. At the top, they all hugged, the animals leaping round them in delight. Sita used her magic to heal Ionie's wound, the deep scratch fading to a pink line and then vanishing completely.

"You were awesome!" Maia told Ionie.

"So brave!" said Sita.

Ionie pushed her hands through her hair.

"I just couldn't let the monkey ruin camp for everyone." She picked up the carved wooden ornament from the ground and shook her head. "I can't believe all the things that have happened were because a spirit was trying to make sure I had a good time!"

"Do you think Miss Amadi knew the monkey had a Jeniyan Spirit in it?" said Lottie.

"No," said Ionie. "Remember it said it was woken up by the touch of Star Magic. I must have done it by accident."

"But when did you touch it?' Lottie asked.

"Miss Amadi put it into my hands," said Ionie. "And told it to make sure I had a good time at camp."

Maia frowned. She thought Miss Amadi had said that and *then* put the monkey in Ionie's hands. *I'm probably remembering it wrong*, she thought.

Sita smiled. "Can you imagine how surprised Miss Amadi would be if she realized she'd started something magical?"

"You don't think there's a chance she knew about the magic, do you?" Maia said slowly.

"Definitely not," said Ionie immediately. "She seemed just as shocked as everyone else when the dens were destroyed and the campfire put out."

"And when our boots went missing," added Lottie.

"If she'd known the monkey was doing those things, I'm sure she'd have tried to stop it," said Sita.

Maia nodded. They were right. And anyway Miss Amadi couldn't have woken up the spirit – it had been Star Magic that had done that.

"We'd better put it back before she notices it's missing," said Ionie.

"OK, but first let's fill the pit in," said Maia. "We don't want anyone else to fall in it!"

They piled soil and branches into the hole and started back to camp.

"We haven't found our team's treasure," Lottie remembered as they walked back along the forest path.

Maia pulled out her mirror. "Cheating might be allowed just this once!"

Using the magic, she found that their treasure box was hidden near the dens. They retrieved it, then hurried back to camp. The animals vanished as they got close.

"Goodness, what happened to you lot?" Miss Amadi said, looking at their muddy hands and dirt-smudged faces.

"And what took you so long? We were just about to send out a search party!" said Connie.

"We … um … fell over," said Maia.

"And got a bit muddy," said Lottie.

Connie laughed. "You certainly did. Well, never mind. You can wash it off in the river this afternoon!"

It was wonderful playing in the river, knowing they'd stopped the Jeniyan Spirit from ruining camp. They swam and splashed in the clear water and then climbed the rocks behind the river, although Ionie stayed on solid ground.

"I am definitely done with climbing today," she told them, sitting on her towel and wriggling her toes in the sun.

The campfire that night was the best yet. They had to pair up with another tent for the quiz about the forest. Maia and the others formed a team with Elissa, Harriet, Anoushka and Maddie. It was fun being with the other girls and Maia was pleased to see Maddie seemed to have made friends with the rest of her tent. Ionie and Lottie answered nearly all the questions but Maddie knew a lot about animals and she was the one who answered the tie-breaking question to win them first prize.

"What is the name for an otter's home?" Miss Amadi asked.

Maddie's hand shot up. "A holt!"

Miss Amadi smiled. "Correct! I declare your team the winners!"

Their prizes were two huge bars of chocolates and badges in the shape of trees to put on their rucksacks.

After the quiz, they had burgers and hot dogs with lots of ketchup and big bowls of salad.

"This has been a brilliant holiday," said Maia happily as she licked her fingers.

"The best!" agreed Lottie.

"We've done so many fun things," said Sita.

Maia nudged Ionie. "So you're glad you didn't go home then?"

Ionie grinned. "Very! It's been awesome!"

Miss Amadi was passing and overheard. "I said you'd have a great time!"

The girls exchanged looks. If only she knew!

After the plates had been cleared away, Connie melted chocolate in a pan over the fire while the rest of the guides handed out strawberries, marshmallows and sticks.

Maia was just making up her second skewer to dip into the melted chocolate when a car drove into the car park and Mrs Coates came walking over to the campfire. Maia's heart sank. They were having so much fun. The last thing they needed was Mrs Coates being grumpy.

"Mrs Coates!" Connie said nervously. "Can I help you?"

To everyone's astonishment, the grey-haired

farmer smiled. "Actually I thought I might be able to help you. I've brought some fresh eggs for your breakfast tomorrow. They're in my car."

"Oh." Connie looked completely taken aback. "Wow, that's very kind of you."

"One good turn deserves another. It was very good of your campers to make those toys and food garlands for my chickens," said Mrs Coates.

"No problem. If it's useful, we can make them as a regular part of the camp programme," said Connie. "Using up food is much better than throwing it away."

Mrs Coates looked pleased. "Thank you. And, if you'd like the campers to see the farm, I'm happy to show them around – and provide you with eggs."

"This is weird. Why's she being so nice?" Maia whispered to Ionie.

"Because of the chicken toys we made – like she said?" suggested Ionie, losing interest in Mrs Coates and turning away to talk to Lottie.

Maia frowned. Making the toys had been a nice idea but was it really enough to have changed Mrs Coates's attitude so dramatically?

Miss Amadi brought a plate of strawberries and marshmallows over to Mrs Coates. "Why don't you join us? It's great when neighbours get on."

"You're right, my dear," said Mrs Coates, sitting down. "And I have to say that ever since you dropped those toys and that raccoon ornament off, I've been feeling differently about this camp."

Maia stiffened. *Raccoon!* They'd been so busy dealing with the monkey that she'd forgotten about the raccoon. Had Miss Amadi given him back to Mrs Coates then?

"I've decided to keep him in my porch with my pot plants," Mrs Coates went on. Maia's eyes widened as she suddenly realised why the plants she'd seen with the raccoon had seemed odd – they were tropical plants not plants you'd get in the forest.

"I've still no idea who left him at my house in the first place, but I'm glad you brought him back." She shook her head. "He's a funny little thing with his big pink acorn, but I do rather like him."

"I'm so pleased," Miss Amadi said. "I was going to keep him but I thought about what it said on the acorn and decided that the right thing to do was to give him back to you as a gift of friendship."

"I wonder where he came from," said Mrs Coates.

Miss Amadi shrugged. "I guess we'll never know."

She clapped her hands to get everyone's attention. "Right, I think it's time for a sing-song!"

As Mrs Coates sat down, Maia frowned. Could the gift of some chicken toys really have changed Mrs Coates' attitude to camp so much? Or could it be something to do with the raccoon? Was there magic at work?

Tom started playing his guitar and Sita slipped her arm through Maia's. "I feel so happy."

"Me too." gave up puzzling about Mrs Coates' change of heart. Maybe it was due to magic, maybe it wasn't. *The important thing is that she seems to have stopped wanting to shut the camp down,* Maia decided.

Ionie stretched. "I can definitely say this is the best camping trip I've ever been on!"

Lottie chuckled. "It's the only camping trip you've ever been on!"

"Yep, and it's the best!" Ionie said with a grin.

Maia looked at her friends. "You know what

would make things even better though?"

"Getting to finally eat our midnight feast tonight?" Lottie said.

"Well, yes, that, of course," said Maia, her eyes sparkling. "But I think it would be better right now if we were somewhere no one could see us." She glanced pointedly at the trees behind them and saw understanding dawning on the others' faces.

Getting up, they all slipped away from the campfire. A few minutes later, they were sitting in their own circle with their animals cuddled beside them.

Gazing at the stars twinkling above them and listening to the music and chatter coming from the campfire, Maia felt a warm rush of happiness. She might not have solved the mystery of the raccoon, but they'd saved the camp and had an amazing time. *A magical time*, she thought, bending down to kiss Bracken's fluffy head. He gave a contented sigh and snuggled even closer into her arms.

Star Friends
Enchanted Mist

Turn the page for a sneak peek of the Star Friends next adventure!

Coming soon...

In the Star World

A snowy owl with silver feathers swooped silently through the forest and came to land on the edge of a rocky pool with a mirror-like surface. The branches of the tall trees around the pool reached up to the star-filled sky, their leaves and trunks glittering. There was a faint rustle as three more animals appeared out of the shadows — a stag, a wolf and a badger. Their fur was tipped with silver and their expressions were wise.

"It appears our four young Star Animals

and their Star Friends from Westcombe have managed to stop magic from causing chaos again," said Hunter the owl, sweeping one wing over the pool. An image of a campfire surrounded by children and adults appeared on the surface. A little way off, nestled against some trees, four girls were cuddling four animals – a young fox, a fallow deer, a red squirrel and a wildcat with a tabby coat. The animals all had indigo eyes just like the wolf, the stag, the badger and the owl. Everyone looked very happy.

"They did well," the wolf said softly. "It helps that they have such a strong friendship."

The others nodded.

"They worked together and stopped people getting hurt," said the stag.

"But they haven't yet realized that there is another Star Animal close by," said Hunter.

The picture changed to show a sleek brown otter with sparkling indigo eyes.

"Fen is inexperienced with Star Magic and needs to learn more. Her Star Friend must also learn not to use other forms of magic unwisely. I hope our young friends will be able to help."

"They need to find Fen first," said the badger.

"Let's hope they do before the magic causes more problems," said the stag.

"Shall we see what happens when they return to Westcombe?" said the wolf.

The others nodded and they all settled down to watch.

Collect Them All!

More from Linda:

When her mum inherits the Curio House, Ava is nervous about moving into the creaky villa, especially when she discovers a room filled with unusual objects and a box of mysterious crystals. And when her mischievous puppy tries to eat one of the artefacts, a series of magical events unfold – and soon the whole town is in trouble!

More from Linda:

Marina is new in Mermaids Rock, having travelled the world with her scientist dad, and she can't wait to make friends! She meets a group of mermaids who love animals and the environment as much as she does and the new friends soon face their first challenge… The beautiful coral caves nearby have been damaged. Who, or what, could have caused the destruction? And why?

More from Linda:

Coralie is overjoyed when she visits a beautiful kelp forest, where she meets adorable sea lions and otters and finds a mysterious treasure map! After telling her friends about it, they're excited to search for the treasure, but when they arrive they find the forest has been destroyed. With no protection from the plants, the animals are in danger, and the friends must do everything they can to save the creatures before it's too late...

More from Linda:

Kai is really excited that Marina is coming to stay while her dad goes on a research trip to the Arctic – they're going to have so much fun! But when they don't hear from him for a few days they start to worry. Travelling through the whirlpool to see if they can find him, the friends are amazed by the icy scene and enchanted by the walruses they meet. But with no sign of Marina's dad and time running out, can the team work together to save the day?

About the Author

Linda Chapman is the best-selling author of over 200 books. The biggest compliment Linda can have is for a child to tell her they became a reader after reading one of her books. Linda lives in a cottage with a tower in Leicestershire with her husband, three children, three dogs and three ponies. When she's not writing, Linda likes to ride, read and visit schools and libraries to talk to people about writing.

www.lindachapmanauthor.co.uk

About the Illustrator

Kim Barnes lives on the Isle of Wight with her partner and two children, Leo and Cameo, who greatly inspire her work. She graduated from Lincoln University, England, and has drawn ever since she was a young child.

www.kimmariaillustration.com